11. JUL 05.

THOMAS HARDY

Selected Poems

BLOOMSBURY
* POETRY *
CLASSICS

This selection by Ian Hamilton first published 1992
Copyright © 1992 by Bloomsbury Publishing Ltd

Bloomsbury Publishing Ltd,
2 Soho Square, London W1V 5DE

A CIP catalogue record for this book
is available from the British Library

ISBN 0 7475 14089

10 9 8 7 6 5 4 3 2 1

Typeset by
Hewer Text Composition Services, Edinburgh
Jacket designed by Jeff Fisher
Printed in Great Britain by
Butler and Tanner Ltd, Frome and London

CONTENTS

5

From *Wessex Poems*

HAP

If but some vengeful god would call to me
From up the sky, and laugh: "Thou suffering thing,
Know that thy sorrow is my ecstasy,
That thy love's loss is my hate's profiting!"

Then I would bear it, clench myself, and die,
Steeled by the sense of ire unmerited;
Half-eased in that a Powerfuller than I
Had willed and meted me the tears I shed.

But not so. How arrives it joy lies slain,
And why unblooms the best hope ever sown?
– Crass Casualty obstructs the sun and rain,
And dicing Time for gladness casts a moan. . . .
These purblind Doomsters had as readily strown
Blisses about my pilgrimage as pain.

NEUTRAL TONES

We stood by a pond that winter day,
And the sun was white, as though chidden of God,
And a few leaves lay on the starving sod;
    – They had fallen from an ash, and were gray.

Your eyes on me were as eyes that rove
Over tedious riddles of years ago;
And some words played between us to and fro
    On which lost the more by our love.

The smile on your mouth was the deadest thing
Alive enough to have strength to die;
And a grin of bitterness swept thereby
    Like an ominous bird a-wing. . . .

Since then, keen lessons that love deceives,
And wrings with wrong, have shaped to me
Your face, and the God-curst sun, and a tree,
    And a pond edged with grayish leaves.

SHE

At His funeral

They bear him to his resting-place –
In slow procession sweeping by;
I follow at a stranger's space;
His kindred they, his sweetheart I.

Unchanged my gown of garish dye,
Though sable-sad is their attire;
But they stand round with griefless eye,
Whilst my regret consumes like fire!

HER DILEMMA

(In — Church)

The two were silent in a sunless church,
Whose mildewed walls, uneven paving-stones,
And wasted carvings passed antique research;
And nothing broke the clock's dull monotones.

Leaning against a wormy poppy-head,
So wan and worn that he could scarcely stand,
 – For he was soon to die, – he softly said,
"Tell me you love me!" – holding long her hand.

She would have given a world to breathe 'yes' truly,
So much his life seemed hanging on her mind,
And hence she lied, her heart persuaded throughly
'Twas worth her soul to be a moment kind.

But the sad need thereof, his nearing death,
So mocked humanity that she shamed to prize
A world conditioned thus, or care for breath
Where Nature such dilemmas could devise.

Perhaps, long hence, when I have passed away,
Some other's feature, accent, thought like mine,
Will carry you back to what I used to say,
And bring some memory of your love's decline.

Then you may pause awhile and think, "Poor jade!"
And yield a sigh to me – as ample due,
Not as the tittle of a debt unpaid
To one who could resign her all to you –

And thus reflecting, you will never see
That your thin thought, in two small words conveyed,
Was no such fleeting phantom-thought to me,
But the Whole Life wherein my part was played;
And you amid its fitful masquerade
A Thought – as I in your life seem to be!

THOUGHTS OF PHENA
At News of Her Death

Not a line of her writing have I,
    Not a thread of her hair,
No mark of her late time as dame in her dwelling,
        whereby
    I may picture her there;
  And in vain do I urge my unsight
    To conceive my lost prize
At her close, whom I knew when her dreams were
        upbrimming with light,
    And with laughter her eyes.

What scenes spread around her last days,
    Sad, shining, or dim?
Did her gifts and compassions enray and enarch her
        sweet ways
    With an aureate nimb?
  Or did life-light decline from her years,
    And mischances control
Her full day-star; unease, or regret, or forebodings, or
        fears
    Disennoble her soul?

Thus I do but the phantom retain
    Of the maiden of yore
As my relic; yet haply the best of her – fined in my
      brain
    It may be the more
  That no line of her writing have I,
    Nor a thread of her hair,
No mark of her late time as dame in her dwelling,
      whereby
    I may picture her there.

I LOOK INTO MY GLASS

I look into my glass,
And view my wasting skin,
And say, "Would God it came to pass
My heart had shrunk as thin!"

For then, I, undistrest
By hearts grown cold to me,
Could lonely wait my endless rest
With equanimity.

But Time, to make me grieve,
Part steals, lets part abide;
And shakes this fragile frame at eve
With throbbings of noontide.

From *Poems of the Past and the Present*

DEPARTURE
(*Southampton Docks: October, 1899*)

While the far farewell music thins and fails,
And the broad bottoms rip the bearing brine –
All smalling slowly to the gray sea-line –
And each significant red smoke-shaft pales,

Keen sense of severance everywhere prevails,
Which shapes the late long tramp of mounting men
To seeming words that ask and ask again:
"How long, O striving Teutons, Slavs, and Gaels

Must your wroth reasonings trade on lives like these,
That are as puppets in a playing hand? –
When shall the saner softer polities
Whereof we dream, have sway in each proud land
And patriotism, grown Godlike, scorn to stand
Bondslave to realms, but circle earth and seas?"

THE GOING OF THE BATTERY
Wives' Lament
(*November 2, 1899*)

I

O it was sad enough, weak enough, mad enough –
Light in their loving as soldiers can be –
First to risk choosing them, leave alone losing them
Now, in far battle, beyond the South Sea! . . .

II

– Rain came down drenchingly; but we unblenchingly
Trudged on beside them through mirk and through
    mire,
They stepping steadily – only too readily! –
Scarce as if stepping brought parting-time nigher.

III

Great guns were gleaming there, living things seeming
    there,
Cloaked in their tar-clothes, upmouthed to the night;
Wheels wet and yellow from axle to felloe,
Throats blank of sound, but prophetic to sight.

IV

Gas-glimmers drearily, blearily, eerily
Lit our pale faces outstretched for one kiss,
While we stood prest to them, with a last quest to
    them
Not to court perils that honour could miss.

V

Sharp were those sighs of ours, blinded these eyes of
    ours,
When at last moved away under the arch
All we loved. Aid for them each woman prayed for
    them,
Treading back slowly the track of their march.

VI

Some one said: "Nevermore will they come: evermore
Are they now lost to us." O it was wrong!
Though may be hard their ways, some Hand will
    guard their ways,
Bear them through safely, in brief time or long.

VII

– Yet, voices haunting us, daunting us, taunting us,
Hint in the night-time when life beats are low
Other and graver things. . . . Hold we to braver things,
Wait we, in trust, what Time's fulness shall show.

DRUMMER HODGE

I

They throw in Drummer Hodge, to rest
    Uncoffined – just as found:
His landmark is a kopje-crest
    That breaks the veldt around;
And foreign constellations west
    Each night above his mound.

II

Young Hodge the Drummer never knew –
    Fresh from his Wessex home –
The meaning of the broad Karoo,
    The Bush, the dusty loam,
And why uprose to nightly view
    Strange stars amid the gloam.

III

Yet portion of that unknown plain
    Will Hodge for ever be;
His homely Northern breast and brain
    Grow to some Southern tree,
And strange-eyed constellations reign
    His stars eternally.

ROME
The Vatican: Sala delle Muse
(1887)

I sat in the Muses' Hall at the mid of the day,
And it seemed to grow still, and the people to pass
   away,
And the chiselled shapes to combine in a haze of sun,
Till beside a Carrara column there gleamed forth One.

She looked not this nor that of those beings divine,
But each and the whole – an essence of all the Nine;
With tentative foot she neared to my halting-place,
A pensive smile on her sweet, small, marvellous face.

"Regarded so long, we render thee sad?" said she.
"Not you," sighed I, "but my own inconstancy!
I worship each and each: in the morning one,
And then, alas! another at sink of sun.

"To-day my soul clasps Form; but where is my troth
Of yesternight with Tune: can one cleave to both?"
– "Be not perturbed," said she. "Though apart in fame,
As I and my sisters are one, those, too, are the same."

– "But my love goes further – to Story, and Dance,
   and Hymn,
The lover of all in a sun-sweep is fool to whim –

Is swayed like a river-weed as the ripples run!"
- "Nay, wooer, thou sway'st not. These are but phases
    of one;

"And that one is I; and I am projected from thee,
One that out of thy brain and heart thou causest to
    be –
Extern to thee nothing. Grieve not, nor thyself becall,
Woo where thou wilt; and rejoice thou canst love at
    all!"

LAUSANNE

In Gibbon's Old Garden: 11–12 p.m.
27 June 1897
(The 110th anniversary of the completion of the 'Decline
and Fall' at the same hour and place)

A Spirit seems to pass,
  Formal in pose, but grave withal and grand:
  He contemplates a volume in his hand,
And far lamps fleck him through the thin acacias.

  Anon the book is closed,
  With "It is finished!" And at the alley's end
  He turns, and when on me his glances bend
As from the Past comes speech – small, muted, yet
      composed.

  "How fares the Truth now? – Ill?
  – Do pens but slily further her advance?
  May one not speed her but in phrase askance?
Do scribes aver the Comic to be Reverend still?

  "Still rule those minds on earth
  At whom sage Milton's wormwood words were
      hurled:
  'Truth like a bastard comes into the world
Never without ill-fame to him who gives her birth'?"

THE BEDRIDDEN PEASANT
To an Unknowing God

Much wonder I – here long low-laid –
   That this dead wall should be
Betwixt the Maker and the made,
   Between Thyself and me!

For, say one puts a child to nurse,
   He eyes it now and then
To know if better it is, or worse,
   And if it mourn, and when.

But Thou, Lord, giv'st us men our day
   In helpless bondage thus
To Time and Chance, and seem'st straightway
   To think no more of us!

That some disaster cleft Thy scheme
   And tore us wide apart,
So that no cry can cross, I deem;
   For Thou art mild of heart,

And wouldst not shape and shut us in
   Where voice can not be heard:
Plainly Thou meant'st that we should win
   Thy succour by a word.

Might but Thy sense flash down the skies
   Like man's from clime to clime,
Thou wouldst not let me agonize
   Through my remaining time;

But, seeing how much Thy creatures bear –
   Lame, starved, or maimed, or blind –
Wouldst heal the ills with quickest care
   Of me and all my kind.

Then, since Thou mak'st not these things be,
   But these things dost not know,
I'll praise Thee as were shown to me
   The mercies Thou wouldst show!

TO LIZBIE BROWNE

I

Dear Lizbie Browne,
Where are you now?
In sun, in rain? –
Or is your brow
Past joy, past pain,
Dear Lizbie Browne?

II

Sweet Lizbie Browne,
How you could smile,
How you could sing! –
How archly wile
In glance-giving,
Sweet Lizbie Browne!

III

And, Lizbie Browne,
Who else had hair
Bay-red as yours,
Or flesh so fair
Bred out of doors,
Sweet Lizbie Browne?

IV

When, Lizbie Browne,
You had just begun
To be endeared
By stealth to one,
You disappeared
My Lizbie Browne!

V

Ay, Lizbie Browne,
So swift your life,
And mine so slow,
You were a wife
Ere I could show
Love, Lizbie Browne.

VI

Still, Lizbie Browne,
You won, they said,
The best of men
When you were wed. . . .
Where went you then,
O Lizbie Browne?

VII

Dear Lizbie Browne,
I should have thought,
"Girls ripen fast,"
And coaxed and caught
You ere you passed,
Dear Lizbie Browne!

VIII

But, Lizbie Browne,
I let you slip;
Shaped not a sign;
Touched never your lip
With lip of mine,
Lost Lizbie Browne!

IX

So, Lizbie Browne,
When on a day
Men speak of me
As not, you'll say,
"And who was he?" –
Yes, Lizbie Browne!

HER REPROACH

Con the dead page as 'twere live love: press on!
Cold wisdom's words will ease thy track for thee;
Aye, go; cast off sweet ways, and leave me wan
To biting blasts that are intent on me.

But if thy object Fame's far summits be,
Whose inclines many a skeleton overlies
That missed both dream and substance, stop and see
How absence wears these cheeks and dims these eyes!

It surely is far sweeter and more wise
To water love, than toil to leave anon
A name whose glory-gleam will but advise
Invidious minds to eclipse it with their own,

And over which the kindliest will but stay
A moment; musing, "He, too, had his day!"

HIS IMMORTALITY

I

I saw a dead man's finer part
Shining within each faithful heart
Of those bereft. Then said I: "This must be
    His immortality."

II

I looked there as the seasons wore,
And still his soul continuously bore
A life in theirs. But less its shine excelled
    Than when I first beheld.

III

His fellow-yearsmen passed, and then
In later hearts I looked for him again;
And found him – shrunk, alas! into a thin
    And spectral mannikin.

IV

Lastly I ask – now old and chill –
If aught of him remain unperished still;
And find, in me alone, a feeble spark,
    Dying amid the dark.

AN AUGUST MIDNIGHT

I

A shaded lamp and a waving blind,
And the beat of a clock from a distant floor:
On this scene enter – winged, horned, and spined –
A longlegs, a moth, and a dumbledore;
While 'mid my page there idly stands
A sleepy fly, that rubs its hands. . . .

II

Thus meet we five, in this still place,
At this point of time, at this point in space.
– My guests besmear my new-penned line,
Or bang at the lamp and fall supine.
"God's humblest, they!" I muse. Yet why?
They know Earth-secrets that know not I.

THE DARKLING THRUSH

I leant upon a coppice gate
   When Frost was spectre-gray,
And Winter's dregs made desolate
   The weakening eye of day.
The tangled bine-stems scored the sky
   Like strings of broken lyres,
And all mankind that haunted nigh
   Had sought their household fires.

The land's sharp features seemed to be
   The Century's corpse outleant,
His crypt the cloudy canopy,
   The wind his death-lament.
The ancient pulse of germ and birth
   Was shrunken hard and dry,
And every spirit upon earth
   Seemed fervourless as I.

At once a voice arose among
   The bleak twigs overhead
In a full-hearted evensong
   Of joy illimited;
An aged thrush, frail, gaunt, and small,
   In blast-beruffled plume,
Had chosen thus to fling his soul
   Upon the growing gloom.

So little cause for carolings
  Of such ecstatic sound
Was written on terrestrial things
  Afar or nigh around,
That I could think there trembled through
  His happy good-night air
Some blessed Hope, whereof he knew
  And I was unaware.

A MAN
(*In Memory of H. of M.*)

I

In Casterbridge there stood a noble pile,
Wrought with pilaster, bay, and balustrade
In tactful times when shrewd Eliza swayed. –
   On burgher, squire, and clown
It smiled the long street down for near a mile.

II

But evil days beset that domicile;
The stately beauties of its roof and wall
Passed into sordid hands. Condemned to fall
   Were cornice, quoin, and cove,
And all that art had wove in antique style.

III

Among the hired dismantlers entered there
One till the moment of his task untold.
When charged therewith he gazed, and answered
    bold:
   "Be needy I or no,
I will not help lay low a house so fair!

IV

"Hunger is hard. But since the terms be such –
No wage, or labour stained with the disgrace
Of wrecking what our age cannot replace

    To save its tasteless soul –
I'll do without your dole. Life is not much!"

V

Dismissed with sneers he packed his tools and went,
And wandered workless; for it seemed unwise
To close with one who dared to criticize

    And carp on points of taste:
Rude men should work where placed, and be content.

VI

Years whiled. He aged, sank, sickened; and was not:
And it was said, "A man intractable
And curst is gone." None sighed to hear his knell,

    None sought his churchyard-place;
His name, his rugged face, were soon forgot.

VII

The stones of that fair hall lie far and wide,
And but a few recall its ancient mould;
Yet when I pass the spot I long to hold

    As truth what fancy saith:
"His protest lives where deathless things abide!"

THE RUINED MAID

"O 'Melia, my dear, this does everything crown!
Who could have supposed I should meet you in Town?
And whence such fair garments, such prosperi-ty?" –
"O didn't you know I'd been ruined?" said she.

– "You left us in tatters, without shoes or socks,
Tired of digging potatoes, and spudding up docks;
And now you've gay bracelets and bright feathers
    three!" –
"Yes: that's how we dress when we're ruined," said
  she.

– "At home in the barton you said 'thee' and 'thou',
And 'thik oon', and 'theäs oon', and 't'other'; but now
Your talking quite fits 'ee for high compa-ny!" –
"Some polish is gained with one's ruin," said she.

– "Your hands were like paws then, your face blue and
    bleak
But now I'm bewitched by your delicate cheek,
And your little gloves fit as on any la-dy!" –
"We never do work when we're ruined," said she.

- "You used to call home-life a hag-ridden dream,
And you'd sigh, and you'd sock; but at present you
  seem
To know not of megrims or melancho-ly!" -
"True. One's pretty lively when ruined," said she.

- "I wish I had feathers, a fine sweeping gown,
And a delicate face, and could strut about Town!" -
"My dear - a raw country girl, such as you be,
Cannot quite expect that. You ain't ruined," said she.

THE SELF-UNSEEING

Here is the ancient floor,
Footworn and hollowed and thin,
Here was the former door
Where the dead feet walked in.

She sat here in her chair,
Smiling into the fire;
He who played stood there,
Bowing it higher and higher.

Childlike, I danced in a dream;
Blessings emblazoned that day;
Everything glowed with a gleam;
Yet we were looking away!

IN TENEBRIS I

"Percussus sum sicut fœnum, et aruit cor meum." – Ps. CI

Wintertime nighs;
But my bereavement-pain
It cannot bring again:
    Twice no one dies.

Flower-petals flee;
But, since it once hath been,
No more that severing scene
    Can harrow me.

Birds faint in dread:
I shall not lose old strength
In the lone frost's black length:
    Strength long since fled!

Leaves freeze to dun;
But friends can not turn cold
This season as of old
    For him with none.

Tempests may scath;
But love can not make smart
Again this year his heart
    Who no heart hath.

Black is night's cope;
But death will not appal
One who, past doubtings all,
Waits in unhope.

TESS'S LAMENT

I

I would that folk forgot me quite,
                Forgot me quite!
I would that I could shrink from sight,
   And no more see the sun.
Would it were time to say farewell,
To claim my nook, to need my knell,
Time for them all to stand and tell
   Of my day's work as done.

II

Ah! dairy where I lived so long,
                I lived so long;
Where I would rise up staunch and strong,
   And lie down hopefully.
'Twas there within the chimney-seat
He watched me to the clock's slow beat –
Loved me, and learnt to call me Sweet,
   And whispered words to me.

III

And now he's gone; and now he's gone; . . .
                And now he's gone!
The flowers we potted perhaps are thrown
   To rot upon the farm.
And where we had our supper-fire

May now grow nettle, dock, and briar,
And all the place be mould and mire
    So cozy once and warm.

IV

And it was I who did it all,
                    Who did it all;
'Twas I who made the blow to fall
    On him who thought no guile.
Well, it is finished – past, and he
Has left me to my misery,
And I must take my Cross on me
    For wronging him awhile.

V

How gay we looked that day we wed,
                    That day we wed!
"May joy be with ye!" they all said
    A-standing by the durn.
I wonder what they say o' us now,
And if they know my lot; and how
She feels who milks my favourite cow,
    And takes my place at churn!

VI

It wears me out to think of it,
                             To think of it;
I cannot bear my fate as writ,
    I'd have my life unbe;
Would turn my memory to a blot,
Make every relic of me rot,
My doings be as they were not,
    And gone all trace of me!

From *Time's Laughingstocks*

ON THE DEPARTURE PLATFORM

We kissed at the barrier; and passing through
She left me, and moment by moment got
Smaller and smaller, until to my view
   She was but a spot;

A wee white spot of muslin fluff
That down the diminishing platform bore
Through hustling crowds of gentle and rough
   To the carriage door.

Under the lamplight's fitful glowers,
Behind dark groups from far and near,
Whose interests were apart from ours,
   She would disappear,

Then show again, till I ceased to see
That flexible form, that nebulous white;
And she who was more than my life to me
   Had vanished quite. . . .

We have penned new plans since that fair fond day,
And in season she will appear again –
Perhaps in the same soft white array –
   But never as then!

- "And why, young man, must eternally fly
A joy you'll repeat, if you love her well?"
- O friend, nought happens twice thus; why,
  I cannot tell!

IN THE VAULTED WAY

In the vaulted way, where the passage turned
To the shadowy corner that none could see,
You paused for our parting, – plaintively;
Though overnight had come words that burned
My fond frail happiness out of me.

And then I kissed you, – despite my thought
That our spell must end when reflection came
On what you had deemed me, whose one long aim
Had been to serve you; that what I sought
Lay not in a heart that could breathe such blame.

But yet I kissed you; whereon you again
As of old kissed me. Why, why was it so?
Do you cleave to me after that light-tongued blow?
If you scorned me at eventide, how love then?
The thing is dark, Dear. I do not know.

THE END OF THE EPISODE

Indulge no more may we
In this sweet-bitter pastime:
The love-light shines the last time
    Between you, Dear, and me.

There shall remain no trace
Of what so closely tied us,
And blank as ere love eyed us
    Will be our meeting-place.

The flowers and thymy air,
Will they now miss our coming?
The dumbles thin their humming
    To find we haunt not there?

Though fervent was our vow,
Though ruddily ran our pleasure,
Bliss has fulfilled its measure,
    And sees its sentence now.

Ache deep; but make no moans:
Smile out; but stilly suffer:
The paths of love are rougher
    Than thoroughfares of stones.

A CHURCH ROMANCE
(*Mellstock: circa 1835*)

She turned in the high pew, until her sight
Swept the west gallery, and caught its row
Of music-men with viol, book, and bow
Against the sinking sad tower-window light.

She turned again; and in her pride's despite
One strenuous viol's inspirer seemed to throw
A message from his string to her below,
Which said: "I claim thee as my own forthright!"

Thus their hearts' bond began, in due time signed.
And long years thence, when Age had scared
   Romance,
At some old attitude of his or glance
That gallery-scene would break upon her mind,
With him as minstrel, ardent, young, and trim,
Bowing "New Sabbath" or "Mount Ephraim".

THE CHRISTENING

Whose child is this they bring
    Into the aisle? –
At so superb a thing
The congregation smile
And turn their heads awhile.

Its eyes are blue and bright,
    Its cheeks like rose;
Its simple robes unite
Whitest of calicoes
With lawn, and satin bows.

A pride in the human race
    At this paragon
Of mortals, lights each face
While the old rite goes on;
But ah, they are shocked anon.

What girl is she who peeps
    From the gallery stair,
Smiles palely, redly weeps,
With feverish furtive air
As though not fitly there?

"I am the baby's mother;
    This gem of the race
The decent fain would smother,
And for my deep disgrace
I am bidden to leave the place."

"Where is the baby's father?" –
    "In the woods afar.
He says there is none he'd rather
Meet under moon or star
Than me, of all that are.

"To clasp me in lovelike weather,
    Wish fixing when,
He says: To be together
At will, just now and then,
Makes him the blest of men;

"But chained and doomed for life
    To slovening
As vulgar man and wife,
He says, is another thing:
Yea: sweet Love's sepulchring!"

NIGHT IN THE OLD HOME

When the wasting embers redden the chimney-breast,
And Life's bare pathway looms like a desert track to
  me,
And from hall and parlour the living have gone to
  their rest,
My perished people who housed them here come back
  to me.

They come and seat them around in their mouldy
  places,
Now and then bending towards me a glance of
  wistfulness,
A strange upbraiding smile upon all their faces,
And in the bearing of each a passive tristfulness.

"Do you uphold me, lingering and languishing here,
A pale late plant of your once strong stock?" I say to
  them;
"A thinker of crooked thoughts upon Life in the sere,
And on That which consigns men to night after
  showing the day to them?"

" – O let be the Wherefore! We fevered our years not
   thus:
Take of Life what it grants, without question!" they
   answer me seemingly.
"Enjoy, suffer, wait: spread the table here freely like us,
And, satisfied, placid, unfretting, watch Time away
   beamingly!"

A WET NIGHT

I pace along, the rain-shafts riddling me,
Mile after mile out by the moorland way,
And up the hill, and through the ewe-leaze gray
Into the lane, and round the corner tree;

Where, as my clothing clams me, mire-bestarred,
And the enfeebled light dies out of day,
Leaving the liquid shades to reign, I say,
"This is a hardship to be calendared!"

Yet sires of mine now perished and forgot,
When worse beset, ere roads were shapen here,
And night and storm were foes indeed to fear,
Times numberless have trudged across this spot
In sturdy muteness on their strenuous lot,
And taking all such toils as trifles mere.

BEFORE LIFE AND AFTER

A time there was – as one may guess
And as, indeed, earth's testimonies tell –
Before the birth of consciousness,
   When all went well.

None suffered sickness, love, or loss,
None knew regret, starved hope, or heart-burnings;
None cared whatever crash or cross
   Brought wrack to things.

If something ceased, no tongue bewailed,
If something winced and waned, no heart was wrung;
If brightness dimmed, and dark prevailed,
   No sense was stung.

But the disease of feeling germed,
And primal rightness took the tinct of wrong;
Ere nescience shall be reaffirmed
   How long, how long?

From *Satires of Circumstance*

AFTER THE VISIT
(*To F.E.D.*)

Come again to the place
Where your presence was as a leaf that skims
Down a drouthy way whose ascent bedims
    The bloom on the farer's face.

Come again, with the feet
That were light on the green as a thistledown ball,
And those mute ministrations to one and to all
    Beyond a man's saying sweet.

Until then the faint scent
Of the bordering flowers swam unheeded away,
And I marked not the charm in the changes of day
    As the cloud-colours came and went.

Through the dark corridors
Your walk was so soundless I did not know
Your form from a phantom's of long ago
    Said to pass on the ancient floors,

Till you drew from the shade,
And I saw the large luminous living eyes
Regard me in fixed inquiring-wise
    As those of a soul that weighed,

    Scarce consciously,
The eternal question of what Life was,
And why we were there, and by whose strange laws
    That which mattered most could not be.

TO MEET, OR OTHERWISE

Whether to sally and see thee, girl of my dreams,
  Or whether to stay
And see thee not! How vast the difference seems
  Of Yea from Nay
Just now. Yet this same sun will slant its beams
  At no far day
On our two mounds, and then what will the
    difference weigh!

Yet I will see thee, maiden dear, and make
  The most I can
Of what remains to us amid this brake
  Cimmerian
Through which we grope, and from whose thorns we
    ache,
  While still we scan
Round our frail faltering progress for some path or
  plan.

By briefest meeting something sure is won;
  It will have been:
Nor God nor Demon can undo the done,
  Unsight the seen,
Make muted music be as unbegun,
  Though things terrene
Groan in their bondage till oblivion supervene.

So, to the one long-sweeping symphony
　　From times remote
Till now, of human tenderness, shall we
　　Supply one note,
Small and untraced, yet that will ever be
　　Somewhere afloat
Amid the spheres, as part of sick Life's antidote.

THE TORN LETTER

I

I tore your letter into strips
  No bigger than the airy feathers
  That ducks preen out in changing weathers
Upon the shifting ripple-tips.

II

In darkness on my bed alone
  I seemed to see you in a vision,
  And hear you say: "Why this derision
Of one drawn to you, though unknown?"

III

Yes, eve's quick mood had run its course,
  The night had cooled my hasty madness;
  I suffered a regretful sadness
Which deepened into real remorse.

IV

I thought what pensive patient days
  A soul must know of grain so tender,
  How much of good must grace the sender
Of such sweet words in such bright phrase.

V

Uprising then, as things unpriced
   I sought each fragment, patched and mended;
   The midnight whitened ere I had ended
And gathered words I had sacrificed.

VI

But some, alas, of those I threw
   Were past my search, destroyed for ever:
   They were your name and place; and never
Did I regain those clues to you.

VII

I learnt I had missed, by rash unheed,
   My track; that, so the Will decided,
   In life, death, we should be divided,
And at the sense I ached indeed.

VIII

That ache for you, born long ago,
   Throbs on: I never could outgrow it.
   What a revenge, did you but know it!
But that, thank God, you do not know.

LOST LOVE

I play my sweet old airs –
   The airs he knew
   When our love was true –
   But he does not balk
   His determined walk,
And passes up the stairs.

I sing my songs once more,
   And presently hear
   His footstep near
   As if it would stay;
   But he goes his way,
And shuts a distant door.

So I wait for another morn,
   And another night
   In this soul-sick blight;
   And I wonder much
   As I sit, why such
A woman as I was born!

AT TEA

The kettle descants in a cosy drone,
And the young wife looks in her husband's face,
And then at her guest's, and shows in her own
Her sense that she fills an envied place;
And the visiting lady is all abloom,
And says there was never so sweet a room.

And the happy young housewife does not know
That the woman beside her was first his choice,
Till the fates ordained it could not be so. . . .
Betraying nothing in look or voice
The guest sits smiling and sips her tea,
And he throws her a stray glance yearningly.

THE DISCOVERY

I wandered to a crude coast
  Like a ghost;
Upon the hills I saw fires –
  Funeral pyres
Seemingly – and heard breaking
Waves like distant cannonades that set the land
  shaking.

And so I never once guessed
  A Love-nest,
Bowered and candle-lit, lay
  In my way,
Till I found a hid hollow,
Where I burst on her my heart could not but follow.

TOLERANCE

"It is a foolish thing," said I,
"To bear with such, and pass it by;
Yet so I do, I know not why!"

And at each cross I would surmise
That if I had willed not in that wise
I might have spared me many sighs.

But now the only happiness
In looking back that I possess –
Whose lack would leave me comfortless –

Is to remember I refrained
From masteries I might have gained,
And for my tolerance was disdained;

For see, a tomb. And if it were
I had bent and broke, I should not dare
To linger in the shadows there.

AT DAY-CLOSE IN NOVEMBER

The ten hours' light is abating,
    And a late bird wings across,
Where the pines, like waltzers waiting,
    Give their black heads a toss.

Beech leaves, that yellow the noon-time,
    Float past like specks in the eye;
I set every tree in my June time,
    And now they obscure the sky.

And the children who ramble through here
    Conceive that there never has been
A time when no tall trees grew here,
    That none will in time be seen.

THE GOING

Why did you give no hint that night
That quickly after the morrow's dawn,
And calmly, as if indifferent quite,
You would close your term here, up and be gone
    Where I could not follow
    With wing of swallow
To gain one glimpse of you ever anon!

    Never to bid good-bye,
    Or lip me the softest call,
Or utter a wish for a word, while I
Saw morning harden upon the wall,
    Unmoved, unknowing
    That your great going
Had place that moment, and altered all.

Why do you make me leave the house
And think for a breath it is you I see
At the end of the alley of bending boughs
Where so often at dusk you used to be;
    Till in darkening dankness
    The yawning blankness
Of the perspective sickens me!

You were she who abode
　By those red-veined rocks far West,
You were the swan-necked one who rode
Along the beetling Beeny Crest,
　And, reining nigh me,
　Would muse and eye me,
While Life unrolled us its very best.

Why, then, latterly did we not speak,
Did we not think of those days long dead,
And ere your vanishing strive to seek
That time's renewal? We might have said,
　"In this bright spring weather
　We'll visit together
Those places that once we visited."

　Well, well! All's past amend,
　Unchangeable. It must go.
I seem but a dead man held on end
To sink down soon. . . . O you could not know
　That such swift fleeing
　No soul foreseeing –
Not even I – would undo me so!

YOUR LAST DRIVE

Here by the moorway you returned,
And saw the borough lights ahead
That lit your face – all undiscerned
To be in a week the face of the dead,
And you told of the charm of that haloed view
That never again would beam on you.

And on your left you passed the spot
Where eight days later you were to lie,
And be spoken of as one who was not;
Beholding it with a heedless eye
As alien from you, though under its tree
You soon would halt everlastingly.

I drove not with you . . . Yet had I sat
At your side that eve I should not have seen
That the countenance I was glancing at
Had a last-time look in the flickering sheen,
Nor have read the writing upon your face,
"I go hence soon to my resting-place;

"You may miss me then. But I shall not know
How many times you visit me there,
Or what your thoughts are, or if you go
There never at all. And I shall not care.
Should you censure me I shall take no heed,
And even your praises no more shall need."

True: never you'll know. And you will not mind.
But shall I then slight you because of such?
Dear ghost, in the past did you ever find
The thought "What profit," move me much?
Yet abides the fact, indeed, the same, –
You are past love, praise, indifference, blame.

THE WALK

You did not walk with me
Of late to the hill-top tree
  By the gated ways,
  As in earlier days;
  You were weak and lame,
  So you never came,
And I went alone, and I did not mind,
Not thinking of you as left behind.

I walked up there to-day
Just in the former way;
  Surveyed around
  The familiar ground
  By myself again;
  What difference, then?
Only that underlying sense
Of the look of a room on returning thence.

THE VOICE

Woman much missed, how you call to me, call to me,
Saying that now you are not as you were
When you had changed from the one who was all to
   me,
But as at first, when our day was fair.

Can it be you that I hear? Let me view you, then,
Standing as when I drew near to the town
Where you would wait for me: yes, as I knew you
   then,
Even to the original air-blue gown!

Or is it only the breeze, in its listlessness
Travelling across the wet mead to me here,
You being ever dissolved to wan wistlessness,
Heard no more again far or near?

   Thus I; faltering forward,
   Leaves around me falling,
Wind oozing thin through the thorn from norward,
   And the woman calling.

AFTER A JOURNEY

Hereto I come to view a voiceless ghost;
   Whither, O whither will its whim now draw me?
Up the cliff, down, till I'm lonely, lost,
   And the unseen waters' ejaculations awe me.
Where you will next be there's no knowing,
   Facing round about me everywhere,
     With your nut-coloured hair,
And gray eyes, and rose-flush coming and going.

Yes: I have re-entered your olden haunts at last;
   Through the years, through the dead scenes I have
      tracked you;
What have you now found to say of our past –
   Scanned across the dark space wherein I have
      lacked you?
Summer gave us sweets, but autumn wrought division?
   Things were not lastly as firstly well
     With us twain, you tell?
But all's closed now, despite Time's derision.

I see what you are doing: you are leading me on
   To the spots we knew when we haunted here
     together,
The waterfall, above which the mist-bow shone
   And the then fair hour in the then fair weather,

And the cave just under, with a voice still so hollow
    That it seems to call out to me from forty years ago,
        When you were all aglow,
And not the thin ghost that I now frailly follow!

Ignorant of what there is flitting here to see,
    The waked birds preen and the seals flop lazily;
Soon you will have, Dear, to vanish from me,
    For the stars close their shutters and the dawn
        whitens hazily.
Trust me, I mind not, though Life lours,
    The bringing me here; nay, bring me here again!
        I am just the same as when
Our days were a joy, and our paths through flowers.

BEENY CLIFF
March 1870–March 1913

I

O the opal and the sapphire of that wandering western
  sea,
And the woman riding high above with bright hair
  flapping free –
The woman whom I loved so, and who loyally loved
  me.

II

The pale mews plained below us, and the waves
  seemed far away
In a nether sky, engrossed in saying their ceaseless
  babbling say,
As we laughed light-heartedly aloft on that clear-
  sunned March day.

III

A little cloud then cloaked us, and there flew an irised
  rain,
And the Atlantic dyed its levels with a dull
  misfeatured stain,
And then the sun burst out again, and purples
  prinked the main.

IV

- Still in all its chasmal beauty bulks old Beeny to the
    sky,
And shall she and I not go there once again now
    March is nigh,
And the sweet things said in that March say anew
    there by and by?

V

What if still in chasmal beauty looms that wild weird
    western shore,
The woman now is – elsewhere – whom the ambling
    pony bore,
And nor knows nor cares for Beeny, and will laugh
    there nevermore.

PLACES

Nobody says: Ah, that is the place
Where chanced, in the hollow of years ago,
What none of the Three Towns cared to know –
The birth of a little girl of grace –
The sweetest the house saw, first or last;
   Yet it was so
   On that day long past.

Nobody thinks: There, there she lay
In a room by the Hoe, like the bud of a flower,
And listened, just after the bedtime hour,
To the stammering chimes that used to play
The quaint Old Hundred-and-Thirteenth tune
   In Saint Andrew's tower
   Night, morn, and noon.

Nobody calls to mind that here
Upon Boterel Hill, where the waggoners skid,
With cheeks whose airy flush outbid
Fresh fruit in bloom, and free of fear,
She cantered down, as if she must fall
   (Though she never did),
   To the charm of all.

Nay: one there is to whom these things,
That nobody else's mind calls back,
Have a savour that scenes in being lack,
And a presence more than the actual brings;
To whom to-day is beneaped and stale,
  And its urgent clack
  But a vapid tale.

From *Moments of Vision*

WE SAT AT THE WINDOW
(*Bournemouth, 1875*)

We sat at the window looking out,
And the rain came down like silken strings
That Swithin's day. Each gutter and spout
Babbled unchecked in the busy way
   Of witless things:
Nothing to read, nothing to see
Seemed in that room for her and me
    On Swithin's day.

We were irked by the scene, by our own selves; yes
For I did not know, nor did she infer
How much there was to read and guess
By her in me, and to see and crown
   By me in her.
Wasted were two souls in their prime,
And great was the waste, that July time
    When the rain came down.

AT THE WICKET-GATE

There floated the sounds of church-chiming,
    But no one was nigh,
Till there came, as a break in the loneness,
    Her father, she, I.
And we slowly moved on to the wicket,
    And downlooking stood,
Till anon people passed, and amid them
    We parted for good.

Greater, wiser, may part there than we three
    Who parted there then,
But never will Fates colder-featured
    Hold sway there again.
Of the churchgoers through the still meadows
    No single one knew
What a play was played under their eyes there
    As thence we withdrew.

HEREDITY

I am the family face;
Flesh perishes, I live on,
Projecting trait and trace
Through time to times anon,
And leaping from place to place
Over oblivion.

The years-heired feature that can
In curve and voice and eye
Despise the human span
Of durance – that is I;
The eternal thing in man,
That heeds no call to die.

YOU WERE THE SORT THAT MEN FORGET

You were the sort that men forget;
    Though I – not yet! –
Perhaps not ever. Your slighted weakness
    Adds to the strength of my regret!

You'd not the art – you never had
    For good or bad –
To make men see how sweet your meaning,
    Which, visible, had charmed them glad.

You would, by words inept let fall,
    Offend them all,
Even if they saw your warm devotion
    Would hold your life's blood at their call.

You lacked the eye to understand
    Those friends off hand
Whose mode was crude, though whose dim purport
    Outpriced the courtesies of the bland.

I am now the only being who
    Remembers you
It may be. What a waste that Nature
    Grudged soul so dear the art its due!

NEAR LANIVET, 1872

There was a stunted handpost just on the crest,
  Only a few feet high:
She was tired, and we stopped in the twilight-time
    for her rest,
  At the crossways close thereby.

She leant back, being so weary, against its stem,
  And laid her arms on its own,
Each open palm stretched out to each end of them,
  Her sad face sideways thrown.

Her white-clothed form at this dim-lit cease of day
  Made her look as one crucified
In my gaze at her from the midst of the dusty way,
  And hurriedly "Don't," I cried.

I do not think she heard. Loosing thence she said,
  As she stepped forth ready to go,
"I am rested now. – Something strange came into my
    head;
  I wish I had not leant so!"

And wordless we moved onward down from the hill
  In the west cloud's murked obscure,
And looking back we could see the handpost still
  In the solitude of the moor.

"It struck her too," I thought, for as if afraid
    She heavily breathed as we trailed;
Till she said, "I did not think how 'twould look in the
        shade,
    When I leant there like one nailed."

I, lightly: "There's nothing in it. For *you*, anyhow!"
    – "O I know there is not," said she . . .
"Yet I wonder. . . . If no one is bodily crucified now,
    In spirit one may be!"

And we dragged on and on, while we seemed to see
    In the running of Time's far glass
Her crucified, as she had wondered if she might be
    Some day. – Alas, alas!

AT MAYFAIR LODGINGS

How could I be aware,
The opposite window eyeing
As I lay listless there,
That through its blinds was dying
One I had rated rare
Before I had set me sighing
For another more fair?

Had the house-front been glass,
My vision unobscuring,
Could aught have come to pass
More happiness-insuring
To her, loved as a lass
When spouseless, all-alluring?
I reckon not, alas!

So, the square window stood,
Steadily night-long shining
In my close neighbourhood,
Who looked forth undivining
That soon would go for good
One there in pain reclining,
Unpardoned, unadieu'd.

Silently screened from view
Her tragedy was ending
That need not have come due
Had she been less unbending.
How near, near were we two
At that last vital rending, –
And neither of us knew!

THE PHOTOGRAPH

The flame crept up the portrait line by line
As it lay on the coals in the silence of the night's
    profound,
  And over the arm's incline,
And along the marge of the silkwork superfine,
And gnawed at the delicate bosom's defenceless
    round.

Then I vented a cry of hurt, and averted my eyes;
The spectacle was one that I could not bear,
  To my deep and sad surprise;
But, compelled to heed, I again looked furtivewise
Till the flame had eaten her breasts, and mouth, and
    hair.

"Thank god, she is out of it now!" I said at last,
In a great relief of heart when the thing was done
  That had set my soul aghast,
And nothing was left of the picture unsheathed from
    the past
But the ashen ghost of the card it had figured on.

She was a woman long hid amid packs of years,
She might have been living or dead; she was lost to
    my sight,
   And the deed that had nigh drawn tears
Was done in a casual clearance of life's arrears;
But I felt as if I had put her to death that night! . . .

 - Well; she knew nothing thereof did she survive,
And suffered nothing if numbered among the dead;
   Yet - yet - if on earth alive
Did she feel a smart, and with vague strange anguish
   strive?
If in heaven, did she smile at me sadly and shake her
   head?

LOVE THE MONOPOLIST
(*Young Lover's Reverie*)

The train draws forth from the station-yard,
  And with it carries me.
I rise, and stretch out, and regard
  The platform left, and see
An airy slim blue form there standing,
  And know that it is she.

While with strained vision I watch on,
  The figure turns round quite
To greet friends gaily; then is gone. . . .
  The import may be slight,
But why remained she not hard gazing
  Till I was out of sight?

"O do not chat with others there,"
  I brood. "They are not I.
O strain your thoughts as if they were
  Gold bands between us; eye
All neighbour scenes as so much blankness
  Till I again am by!

"A troubled soughing in the breeze
  And the sky overhead
Let yourself feel; and shadeful trees,
  Ripe corn, and apples red,
Read as things barren and distasteful
  While we are separated!

"When I come back uncloak your gloom,
  And let in lovely day;
Then the long dark as of the tomb
  Can well be thrust away
With sweet things I shall have to practise,
  And you will have to say!"

ON STURMINSTER FOOT-BRIDGE
(Onomatopœic)

Reticulations creep upon the slack stream's face
   When the wind skims irritably past,
The current clucks smartly into each hollow place
That years of flood have scrabbled in the pier's
     sodden base;
   The floating-lily leaves rot fast.

On a roof stand the swallows ranged in wistful
     waiting rows,
   Till they arrow off and drop like stones
Among the eyot-withies at whose foot the river flows:
And beneath the roof is she who in the dark world
     shows
   As a lattice-gleam when midnight moans.

LOGS ON THE HEARTH
A Memory of a Sister

The fire advances along the log
    Of the tree we felled,
Which bloomed and bore striped apples by the
      peck
    Till its last hour of bearing knelled.

The fork that first my hand would reach
    And then my foot
In climbings upward inch by inch, lies now
    Sawn, sapless, darkening with soot.

Where the bark chars is where, one year,
    It was pruned, and bled –
Then overgrew the wound. But now, at last,
    Its growings all have stagnated.

My fellow-climber rises dim
    From her chilly grave –
Just as she was, her foot near mine on the
      bending limb,
    Laughing, her young brown hand awave.

DURING WIND AND RAIN

They sing their dearest songs –
He, she, all of them – yea,
Treble and tenor and bass,
        And one to play;
With the candles mooning each face. . . .
        Ah, no; the years O!
How the sick leaves reel down in throngs!

They clear the creeping moss –
Elders and juniors – aye,
Making the pathways neat
        And the garden gay;
And they build a shady seat. . . .
        Ah, no; the years, the years;
See, the white storm-birds wing across!

They are blithely breakfasting all –
Men and maidens – yea,
Under the summer tree,
        With a glimpse of the bay,
While pet fowl come to the knee. . . .
        Ah, no; the years O!
And the rotten rose is ript from the wall.

They change to a high new house,
He, she, all of them – aye,
Clocks and carpets and chairs
    On the lawn all day,
And brightest things that are theirs. . . .
    Ah, no; the years, the years;
Down their carved names the rain-drop
        ploughs.

HE PREFERS HER EARTHLY

This after-sunset is a sight for seeing,
Cliff-heads of craggy cloud surrounding it.
    – And dwell you in that glory-show?
You may; for there are strange strange things in being,
    Stranger than I know.

Yet if that chasm of splendour claim your presence
Which glows between the ash cloud and the dun,
    How changed must be your mortal mould!
Changed to a firmament-riding earthless essence
    From what you were of old:

All too unlike the fond and fragile creature
Then known to me. . . . Well, shall I say it plain?
    I would not have you thus and there,
But still would grieve on, missing you, still feature
    You as the one you were.

AN UPBRAIDING

Now I am dead you sing to me
   The songs we used to know,
But while I lived you had no wish
   Or care for doing so.

Now I am dead you come to me
   In the moonlight, comfortless;
Ah, what would I have given alive
   To win such tenderness!

When you are dead, and stand to me
   Not differenced, as now,
But like again, will you be cold
   As when we lived, or how?

IN TIME OF "THE BREAKING OF NATIONS"

I

Only a man harrowing clods
   In a slow silent walk
With an old horse that stumbles and nods
   Half asleep as they stalk.

II

Only thin smoke without flame
   From the heaps of couch-grass;
Yet this will go onward the same
   Though Dynasties pass.

III

Yonder a maid and her wight
   Come whispering by:
War's annals will cloud into night
   Ere their story die.

AFTERWARDS

When the Present has latched its postern behind my
    tremulous stay,
  And the May month flaps its glad green leaves like
    wings,
Delicate-filmed as new-spun silk, will the neighbours
    say,
  "He was a man who used to notice such things"?

If it be in the dusk when, like an eyelid's soundless
    blink,
  The dewfall-hawk comes crossing the shades to
    alight
Upon the wind-warped upland thorn, a gazer may
    think,
  "To him this must have been a familiar sight."

If I pass during some nocturnal blackness, mothy and
    warm,
  When the hedgehog travels furtively over the
    lawn,
One may say, "He strove that such innocent creatures
    should come to no harm,
  But he could do little for them; and now he is
    gone."

If, when hearing that I have been stilled at last, they
      stand at the door,
   Watching the full-starred heavens that winter sees,
Will this thought rise on those who will meet my face
      no more,
   "He was one who had an eye for such mysteries"?

And will any say when my bell of quittance is heard
      in the gloom,
   And a crossing breeze cuts a pause in its
      outrollings,
Till they rise again, as they were a new bell's boom,
   "He hears it not now, but used to notice such
      things"?

From *Late Lyrics*

WEATHERS

I

This is the weather the cuckoo likes,
   And so do I;
When showers betumble the chestnut spikes,
   And nestlings fly:
And the little brown nightingale bills his best,
And they sit outside at "The Travellers' Rest",
And maids come forth sprig-muslin drest,
And citizens dream of the south and west,
   And so do I.

II

This is the weather the shepherd shuns,
   And so do I;
When beeches drip in browns and duns,
   And thresh, and ply;
And hill-hid tides throb, throe on throe,
And meadow rivulets overflow,
And drops on gate-bars hang in a row,
And rooks in families homeward go,
   And so do I.

A WET AUGUST

Nine drops of water bead the jessamine,
And nine-and-ninety smear the stones and tiles:
 – 'Twas not so in that August – full-rayed, fine –
When we lived out-of-doors, sang songs, strode miles.

Or was there then no noted radiancy
Of summer? Were dun clouds, a dribbling bough,
Gilt over by the light I bore in me,
And was the waste world just the same as now?

It can have been so: yea, that threatenings
Of coming down-drip on the sunless gray,
By the then golden chances seen in things
Were wrought more bright than brightest skies
    to-day.

THE OLD GOWN
(Song)

I have seen her in gowns the brightest,
    Of azure, green, and red,
And in the simplest, whitest,
    Muslined from heel to head;
I have watched her walking, riding,
    Shade-flecked by a leafy tree,
Or in fixed thought abiding
    By the foam-fingered sea.

In woodlands I have known her,
    When boughs were mourning loud,
In the rain-reek she has shown her
    Wild-haired and watery-browed.
And once or twice she has cast me
    As she pomped along the street
Court-clad, ere quite she had passed me,
    A glance from her chariot-seat.

But in my memoried passion
    For evermore stands she
In the gown of fading fashion
    She wore that night when we,

Doomed long to part, assembled
In the snug small room; yea, when
She sang with lips that trembled,
"Shall I see his face again?"

WHERE THREE ROADS JOINED

Where three roads joined it was green and fair,
And over a gate was the sun-glazed sea,
And life laughed sweet when I halted there;
Yet there I never again would be.

I am sure those branchways are brooding now,
With a wistful blankness upon their face,
While the few mute passengers notice how
Spectre-beridden is the place;

Which nightly sighs like a laden soul,
And grieves that a pair, in bliss for a spell
Not far from thence, should have let it roll
Away from them down a plumbless well

While the phasm of him who fared starts up,
And of her who was waiting him sobs from near
As they haunt there and drink the wormwood cup
They filled for themselves when their sky was clear.

Yes, I see those roads – now rutted and bare,
While over the gate is no sun-glazed sea;
And though life laughed when I halted there,
It is where I never again would be.

"AND THERE WAS A GREAT CALM"
(On the Signing of the Armistice, 11 Nov. 1918)

I

There had been years of Passion – scorching, cold,
And much Despair, and Anger heaving high,
Care whitely watching, Sorrows manifold,
Among the young, among the weak and old,
And the pensive Spirit of Pity whispered, "Why?"

II

Men had not paused to answer. Foes distraught
Pierced the thinned peoples in a brute-like blindness,
Philosophies that sages long had taught,
And Selflessness, were as an unknown thought,
And "Hell!" and "Shell!" were yapped at
   Lovingkindness.

III

The feeble folk at home had grown full-used
To "dug-outs", "snipers", "Huns", from the war-adept
In the mornings heard, and at evetides perused;
To day-dreamt men in millions, when they mused –
To nightmare-men in millions when they slept.

IV

Waking to wish existence timeless, null,
Sirius they watched above where armies fell;
He seemed to check his flapping when, in the lull
Of night a boom came thencewise, like the dull
Plunge of a stone dropped into some deep well.

V

So, when old hopes that earth was bettering slowly
Were dead and damned, there sounded "War is done!"
One morrow. Said the bereft, and meek, and lowly,
"Will men some day be given to grace? yea, wholly,
And in good sooth, as our dreams used to run?"

VI

Breathless they paused. Out there men raised their
    glance
To where had stood those poplars lank and lopped,
As they had raised it through the four years' dance
Of Death in the now familiar flats of France;
And murmured, "Strange, this! How? All firing
    stopped?"

VII

Aye; all was hushed. The about-to-fire fired not,
The aimed-at moved away in trance-lipped song.
Our checkless regiment slung a clinching shot
And turned. The Spirit of Irony smirked out, "What?
Spoil peradventures woven of Rage and Wrong?"

VIII

Thenceforth no flying fires inflamed the gray,
No hurtlings shook the dewdrop from the thorn,
No moan perplexed the mute bird on the spray;
Worn horses mused: "We are not whipped to-day;"
No weft-winged engines blurred the moon's thin horn.

IX

Calm fell. From Heaven distilled a clemency;
There was peace on earth, and silence in the sky;
Some could, some could not, shake off misery:
The Sinister Spirit sneered: "It had to be!"
And again the Spirit of Pity whispered, "Why?"

IF IT'S EVER SPRING AGAIN
(Song)

If it's ever spring again,
  Spring again,
I shall go where went I when
Down the moor-cock splashed, and hen,
Seeing me not, amid their flounder,
Standing with my arm around her;
If it's ever spring again,
  Spring again,
I shall go where went I then.

If it's ever summer-time,
  Summer-time,
With the hay crop at the prime,
And the cuckoos – two – in rhyme,
As they used to be, or seemed to,
We shall do as long we've dreamed to,
If it's ever summer-time,
  Summer-time,
With the hay, and bees achime.

From *Human Shows*

SNOW IN THE SUBURBS

Every branch big with it,
    Bent every twig with it;
Every fork like a white web-foot;
Every street and pavement mute:
Some flakes have lost their way, and grope back
        upward, when
Meeting those meandering down they turn and
        descend again.
The palings are glued together like a wall,
And there is no waft of wind with the fleecy fall.

A sparrow enters the tree,
    Whereon immediately
A snow-lump thrice his own slight size
Descends on him and showers his head and eyes,
    And overturns him,
    And near inurns him,
And lights on a nether twig, when its brush
Starts off a volley of other lodging lumps with a rush.

The steps are a blanched slope,
Up which, with feeble hope,
A black cat comes, wide-eyed and thin;
    And we take him in.

NO BUYERS
A Street Scene

A Load of brushes and baskets and cradles and
    chairs
  Labours along the street in the rain:
With it a man, a woman, a pony with whiteybrown
  hairs. –
  The man foots in front of the horse with a
    shambling sway
    At a slower tread than a funeral train,
  While to a dirge-like tune he chants his wares,
Swinging a Turk's-head brush (in a drum-major's way
    When the bandsmen march and play).

A yard from the back of the man is the whiteybrown
    pony's nose:
He mirrors his master in every item of pace and pose:
    He stops when the man stops, without being
    told,
  And seems to be eased by a pause; too plainly he's
    old,
    Indeed, not strength enough shows
    To steer the disjointed waggon straight,
  Which wriggles left and right in a rambling line,
  Deflected thus by its own warp and weight,
  And pushing the pony with it in each incline.

The woman walks on the pavement verge,
    Parallel to the man:
She wears an apron white and wide in span,
And carries a like Turk's-head, but more in nursing-wise:
    Now and then she joins in his dirge,
    But as if her thoughts were on distant things.
    The rain clams her apron till it clings. –
So, step by step, they move with their merchandize,
    And nobody buys.

WHEN OATS WERE REAPED

That day when oats were reaped, and wheat was
      ripe, and barley ripening,
  The road-dust hot, and the bleaching grasses dry,
    I walked along and said,
While looking just ahead to where some silent people
      lie:

"I wounded one who's there, and now know well I
      wounded her;
  But, ah, she does not know that she wounded me!"
    And not an air stirred,
Nor a bill of any bird; and no response accorded she.

THE HARBOUR BRIDGE

From here, the quay, one looks above to mark
The bridge across the harbour, hanging dark
Against the day's-end sky, fair-green in glow
Over and under the middle archway's bow:
It draws its skeleton where the sun has set,
Yea, clear from cutwater to parapet;
On which mild glow, too, lines of rope and spar
    Trace themselves black as char.

Down here in shade we hear the painters shift
Against the bollards with a drowsy lift,
As moved by the incoming stealthy tide.
High up across the bridge the burghers glide
As cut black-paper portraits hastening on
In conversation none knows what upon:
Their sharp-edged lips move quickly word by word
    To speech that is not heard.

There trails the dreamful girl, who leans and stops,
There presses the practical woman to the shops,
There is a sailor, meeting his wife with a start,
And we, drawn nearer, judge they are keeping apart.

Both pause. She says: "I've looked for you. I thought
We'd make it up." Then no words can be caught.
At last: "Won't you come home?" She moves still
    nigher:
  " 'Tis comfortable, with a fire."

"No," he says gloomily. "And, anyhow,
I can't give up the other woman now:
You should have talked like that in former days,
When I was last home." They go different ways.
And the west dims, and yellow lamplights shine:
And soon above, like lamps more opaline,
White stars ghost forth, that care not for men's wives,
    Or any other lives.

THE THING UNPLANNED

The white winter sun struck its stroke on the bridge,
  The meadow-rills rippled and gleamed
As I left the thatched post-office, just by the ridge,
And dropped in my pocket her long tender letter,
With: "This must be snapped! it is more than it
    seemed;
  And now is the opportune time!"

But against what I willed worked the surging sublime
  Of the thing that I did – the thing better!

From *Winter Words*

LYING AWAKE

You, Morningtide Star, now are steady-eyed, over
    the east,
  I know it as if I saw you;
You, Beeches, engrave on the sky your thin twigs,
    even the least;
  Had I paper and pencil I'd draw you.

You, Meadow, are white with your counterpane
    cover of dew,
  I see it as if I were there;
You, Churchyard, are lightening faint from the shade
    of the yew,
  The names creeping out everywhere.

HE NEVER EXPECTED MUCH
[or]
A Consideration
[*A reflection*] *on My Eighty-Sixth Birthday*

Well, World, you have kept faith with me,
    Kept faith with me;
Upon the whole you have proved to be
    Much as you said you were.
Since as a child I used to lie
Upon the leaze and watch the sky,
Never, I own, expected I
    That life would all be fair.

'Twas then you said, and since have said,
    Times since have said,
In that mysterious voice you shed
    From clouds and hills around:
"Many have loved me desperately,
Many with smooth serenity,
While some have shown contempt of me
    Till they dropped underground.

"I do not promise overmuch,
    Child; overmuch;
Just neutral-tinted haps and such,"
    You said to minds like mine.
Wise warning for your credit's sake!
Which I for one failed not to take,
And hence could stem such strain and ache
    As each year might assign.

Uncollected

THEY ARE GREAT TREES

They are great trees, no doubt, by now,
 That were so thin in bough –
  That row of limes –
When we housed there; I'm loth to reckon when;
 The world has turned so many times,
  So many, since then!